To the Leon brothers, Ricardo and José Luis,
who taught me a lot about Ecuador and dancing —*M.S.*

For Victoria Wells Arms, with great appreciation —*S.L.R.*

AUTHOR'S NOTE AND ACKNOWLEDGMENTS

Researching and writing this book has been a wonderful journey. Besides reading many articles, primarily online, and several books, I had the rare pleasure of consulting with people from or knowledgeable about the cultures, religions, and countries represented. They live in places as far away as New Zealand and India and as near as Brooklyn, New York. I am incredibly grateful to all of them for their help and insights into Russian, Scottish, Chinese, Persian, Thai, Muslim, Māori, Mapuche, Parsi, Kemetic, Ethiopian, Jewish, Hindu, Spanish, and Ecuadorian New Year celebrations. Here are their names and, in some cases, websites: Sumbul Ali-Karamali (http://www.muslimnextdoor.com); Davar Ardalan (http://www. civicjournalist.com/); Seleshi Ayalew Asfaw, Executive Director, and Laura Berger, Director of Development, Ethiopian Tewahedo Social Services (ETSS) (http:// www.ethiotss.org); Nicolás Canales, Spanish Blackbelt Founder (http://www. spanishblackbelt.com); Teresa Chung, Administrator, Thai Community Arts and Cultural Center (TCACC) (http://thaiculturalcenter.org/default.htm); Rabbi Dena Feingold (http://www.bethhillel.net); Sonia Gilbukh; Wendi Gu; Jennifer Horsburgh; Uma Krishnaswami (http://umakrishnaswami.org); José Luis Leon; Ricardo Leon; Ana Lopez; Xing Lu; Gertrudis Masch; Sheena Matthews; Heraldo Muñoz, Assistant Secretary General, Assistant Administrator, and Regional Director for Latin America and the Caribbean of the United Nations Development Programme (http://www. latinamerica.undp.org/content/undp/en/home/); Barbara Olguin (www.opentravel. cl); Zakkiya Osman (http://muslimmommy.com); Gaston Otero-Frauwallner (http:// mapuche.com); Khola Pasha; Umama Pasha; Haneta Pierce, former Team Leader, Māori Services, Christchurch City Libraries (http://my.christchurchcitylibraries.com/ te-ao-maori/); Emma Pollock, Marketing and Public Relations Manager (http:// www.scotland.org/us/); Ruamporn Ridthiprasart, former First Secretary, Protocol, Press, Cultural, and Educational Affairs, Royal Thai Embassy, Ottawa, Canada (http:// www.thaiembassy.ca/en); Aban Rustomji, Webmaster, FIRES: FEZANA Information Research Education System (http://fires-fezana.org); Thanyaphorn Saiphan; Amy Shah; Rima S. Shah (http://divaayurveda.com); Saryu Shah; Medeia Sharif (http:// www.medeiasharif.com); Laurie Shayler; Tamara L. Siuda, Egyptologist (http:// tamarasiuda.com); Desta Sium, Roots Ethiopia (http://www.rootsethiopia.org); Sarduriur Freydis Sverresdatter (https://warboar.wordpress.com/about/); Yazdi Tantra (http://zoroastrians.net/contact-us/); Homa S. Tavangar (http://www. growingupglobal.net); Habtemaryam Fentaw Teklu (http://awazetours.com/index. html); Meghan Walsh, Founder, Roots Ethiopia; Vibul Wonprasat, Artistic Director, TCACC; Natasha Zaitseff; and Zahra Ziani.

ILLUSTRATOR'S NOTE AND ACKNOWLEDGMENTS

Remembering Jean Robbins and music-filled Happy New Years. And special thank-yous to Eva Eakin and Leo Eakin, studio assistants and handmade paper makers, and to Nancy Patz, for that which she does.

LEE & LOW BOOKS INC., 95 Madison Avenue, New York, NY 10016, leeandlow.com
Edited by Louise E. May
Designed by Christy Hale
Production by The Kids at Our House
The text is set in Rotis San Serif
The collage illustrations are created from papers collected all over the world
Manufactured in China by Jade Productions, March 2018
Printed on paper from responsible sources
10 9 8 7 6 5 4 3 2 1
First Edition

Library of Congress Cataloging-in-Publication Data
Names: Singer, Marilyn, author. | Roth, Susan L., illustrator.
Title: Every month is a new year : celebrations around the world / poems by Marilyn Singer ; collages by Susan L. Roth.
Description: First edition. | New York : Lee & Low Books Inc., [2017]
Identifiers: LCCN 2016027055 | ISBN 9781620141625 (hardcover : acid-free paper)
Subjects: LCSH: New Year—Poetry.
Classification: LCC PS3569.I546 A6 2017 | DDC 811/.54—dc23
LC record available at https://lccn.loc.gov/2016027055

EVERY MONTH IS A NEW YEAR

Celebrations Around the World

poems by MARILYN SINGER

collages by SUSAN L. ROTH

Lee & Low Books Inc.   New York

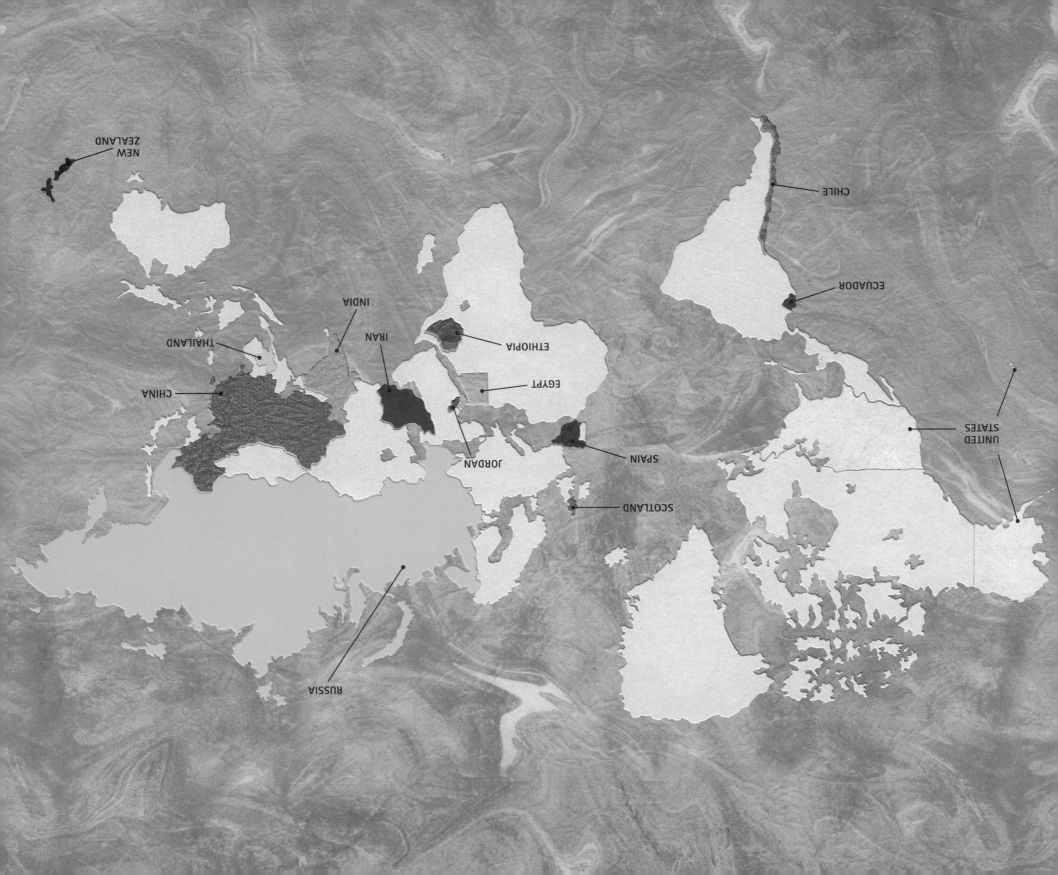

HAPPY NEW YEAR!

All around the world, people celebrate New Year's Day beginning at midnight when December 31 becomes January 1. They ring out the old year and ring in the new with a variety of festivities that include eating and drinking holiday foods and beverages, shooting off fireworks, blaring horns, beating drums, giving gifts, dancing, making resolutions, or actually ringing bells.

But January 1 is not the only day that the new year is celebrated. Chinese New Year, also known as the Spring Festival, falls sometime in January or February. Nowruz, the Iranian New Year, begins in March, when spring begins in the Northern Hemisphere. In Thailand, festivities for Songkran are held from April 13 to 15. The Jewish New Year, Rosh Hashanah, occurs in September or October, and it begins at sunset. Diwali, celebrated in parts of India, starts at sunrise on a day in October or November. The date of the Islamic New Year varies from year to year, but it always begins at the first sighting of a crescent moon.

Some of these celebrations are secular, not religious. Others are religious. And still others have religious roots but are combined with secular traditions. Iranians set a table with seven special dishes with names that begin with the letter *s* (*seen*) in Persian. Thai people hold what is perhaps the world's biggest water fight. Hindus light lamps and bonfires. Muslims spend the day quietly in prayer. Jews go to synagogue to worship, and some practice *tashlich*, casting away sins (in the form of pebbles or bits of bread) into a body of water. Spaniards eat twelve grapes for good luck.

No matter how they celebrate or on what date, people everywhere find a time to wish one another "Happy New Year." Come along and rejoice!

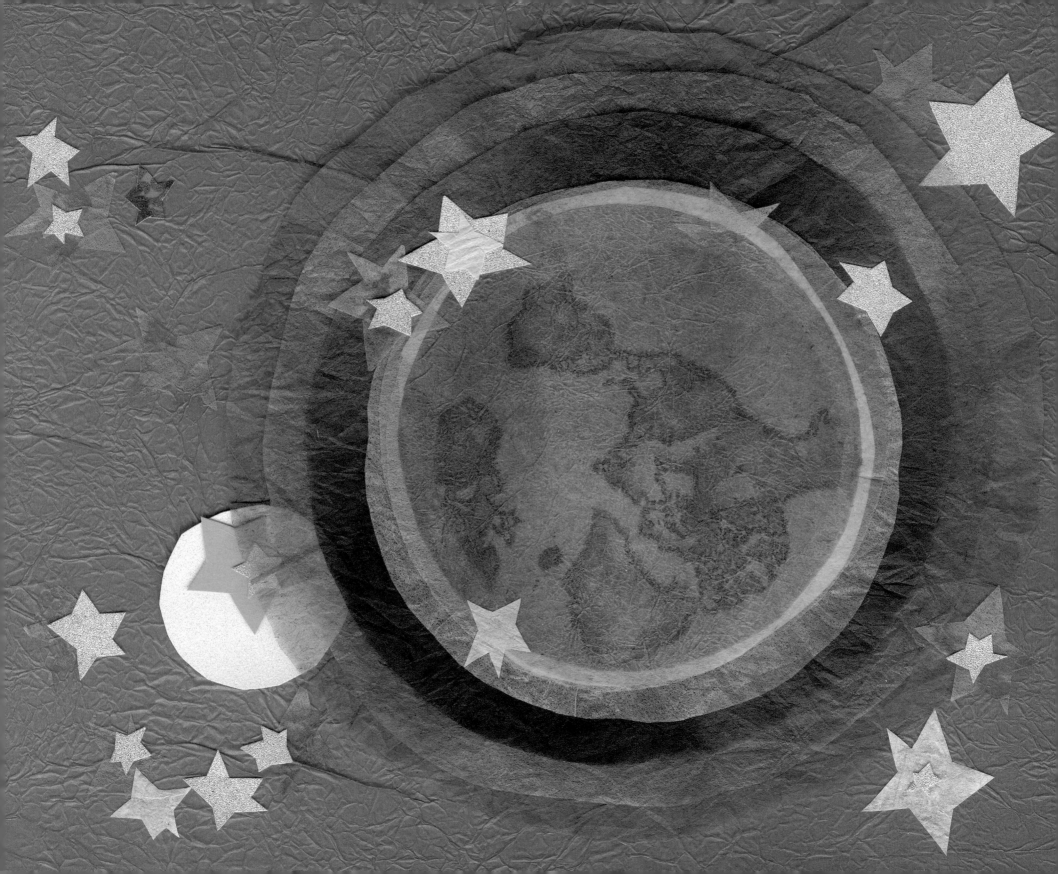

THE YEAR TURNS

We choose the date.
From the earth's movement,
from the moon's phases,
these clocks and calendars
we create.
Together
in parks and squares,
in temples and houses—
watching
the year
turn,
we
celebrate.

DECEMBER

MIDNIGHT BALL DROP

NEW YEAR'S EVE
New York City, United States

Tonight,
hand in hand with
Grandma, I stand in the
middle of this merry, loud crowd
waiting

for that
glittering ball
to drop at the magic
hour, bringing on a confetti
shower

over
Times Square. My friends
may say they saw it on
TV, but I can brag that I
was there!

FIRST FOOTING

HOGMANAY
Scotland

Midnight! And the bells are ringing!
"Auld Lang Syne"—they're downstairs, singing!
We're supposed to be in bed,
    but we're peeking out instead
        to see what First Footer
           will come our way
with grown-up treats and great good luck
    tonight on Hogmanay.
Will it be a stranger,
    tall, with hair that's dark?
Ooh, there's someone knocking!
    It's our short, bald uncle Mark!
We run out to hug him,
    and we're allowed to stay
to greet the year with gifts and cheer
    tonight on Hogmanay.

DECEMBER-JANUARY

TWO NEW YEARS

RUSSIAN NEW YEARS
Russia

The fir tree is up,
and we are arguing this "New" New Year's Eve
        about where to hang the ornaments.
Grandfather Frost here? Snow Maiden there?
We want this tree to be perfect
        right through the "Old" New Year's Day,
                two whole weeks from now.
Then Babushka marches into the room,
        gently shaking her head.
"You silly children do not know how lucky you are
        to celebrate twice.
Two New Years (and Christmas too),
        what more can you want?"
For a moment, we do not say a word.
Then my sister picks up the star,
        and I place it on the tip-top of the tree.
And with our arms around each other,
        we both agree it is

                        perfect.

FEBRUARY

DRAGON DANCE

CHINESE NEW YEAR

Hong Kong, China

Today my shy brother
    has become part red dragon,
        dancing joyfully in the square,
        whipping his tail to the beat, beat of the drum,
        chasing away the evil spirits,
        bringing health, wealth, joy.
"Gong hey fat choy!" I cry
    as he passes by.
Later at our family feast
    we will have dumplings, oranges, long noodles,
        and more.
And my shy brother,
    who had been part glorious beast,
        will not give the smallest roar.

THIRTEEN DAYS

NOWRUZ
Iran

The house is clean.
The seeds are sprouting.
We'll set the haft seen.
We'll go on an outing
    to sit beneath pistachio trees,
    greening in the fresh March breeze.
At home, in new dresses, new shoes,
    and new suits,
we'll sit by the table
    with pudding and fruits,
    with flowers and goldfish,
    with sabzeh and seer.
We'll kiss and we'll hug,
    wishing all a good year.
On the thirteenth day
    we'll visit the park,
play in the sunlight, banish the dark,
    get rid of the sabzeh (and with it, bad news).
The world is reborn
    every spring on Nowruz.

WASHING THE BAD AWAY

SONGKRAN

Thailand

Three hot days in April.
Time to scrub the house.
Time to bathe the Buddhas,
    to build stupas out of sand,
        so we gather blessings, so we understand
how good deeds make our lives complete.
Time to pour into the street
    with buckets, bottles, water guns,
        to splash everyone in sight,
        to be sprayed by elephants,
            fire engines,
            the people we meet,
    to start the new year right
with a gigantic water fight.

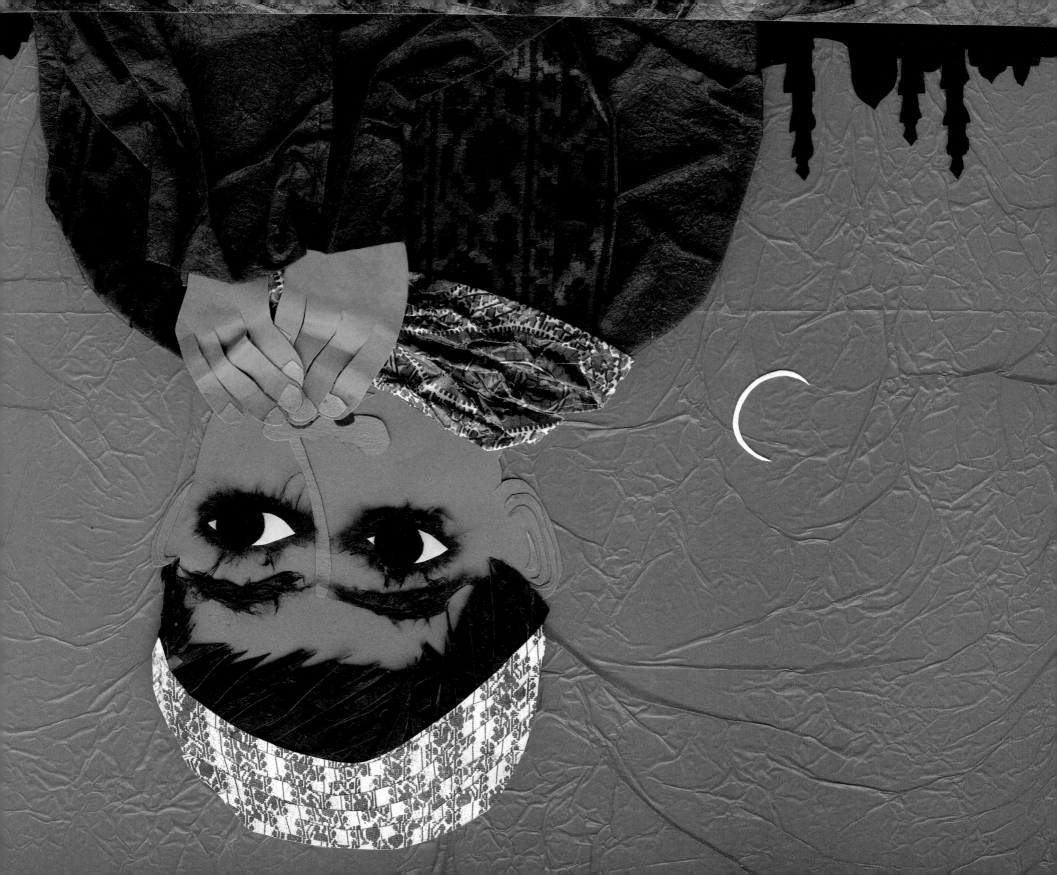

MAY

NEW MOON, NEW YEAR

FIRST DAY OF MUHARRAM
Jordan

My brother has heard this solemn story before—
of the Prophet's ☪ passage,
of how our community began—
but not in the masjid.
Going to the mosque is as new to him
as the crescent moon.
My brother does not need fireworks
to make his eyes sparkle.
Surrounded by peace and prayer,
he is bright with this new year,
he is aglow with growing up.

JUNE

BRINGING TOGETHER EARTH AND SKY

MATARIKI
New Zealand

When the Little Eyes
rise,
heralding the new year,
we will talk of who came before us,
we will know our bones,
we will send our kite
toward those stars—
the sacred seven.
We will watch it fly to heaven,
uniting Earth and sky.
My sister will wonder,
"Can we make it go that high?"
My answer will be,
"Now is the best time to try!"

THE YOUNG SUN RISES

WE TRIPANTU
Chile

The night is cold.
My family is warm
    with stories of new years past.
The air is quiet.
My family is loud
    with music on the flute, horn, drum,
    and laughter all around.
Winter has begun.
But dawn will come.
Together we will stand in the doorway.
Together we will shout,
    "¡Wiñoi Tripantu!"
to the young sun.
And around the rewe
    we will dance.
Oh how we will dance!

JULY

SMASHING THE POTS

WEP RONPET

United States/Ancient Egypt

Everyone believes in a different beginning.
The year may start for me, for you, anew
    in January, April, May,
or in some other month, on some other day.
In Egypt, long ago
    it began when people prayed
        the Nile would perfectly overflow
at the start of Akhet
    as Sopdet rose just before the sun,
and the land would be made fertile—
    there would be food for everyone.
Even now some are sure
    this is the time all is made pure,
with taking baths or cleansing showers,
with cleaning out the house,
with putting setbacks and strife onto red pots
and smashing them to pieces
so that goodness increases
    and harmony is once again winning.
Everyone believes in a different beginning.
But what is true and what is clear
    is that all of us hope for a luminous year.

NOWRUZ, NAVROZE

NAVROZE
India

"Nowruz, Navroze. Call it what you wish,"
    says my cousin from Iran,
piling his plate with pulao, his favorite dish.
    How he loves his rice!
"Navroze, Nowruz. So nice we celebrate it twice,"
    I say, and pass him fish in banana leaves,
    lentils cooked with ghee.
Yes, the year begins in March for him,
    in August for me—
    (though the hour it starts will vary).
Picturing his haft seen table, my visit to the agiary,
    breathing in the sandalwood,
    watching the temple's sacred flame
    sending prayers of peace for all,
I believe no matter the name—
    what lips may say a different way,
    hearts will call the same.

SEPTEMBER

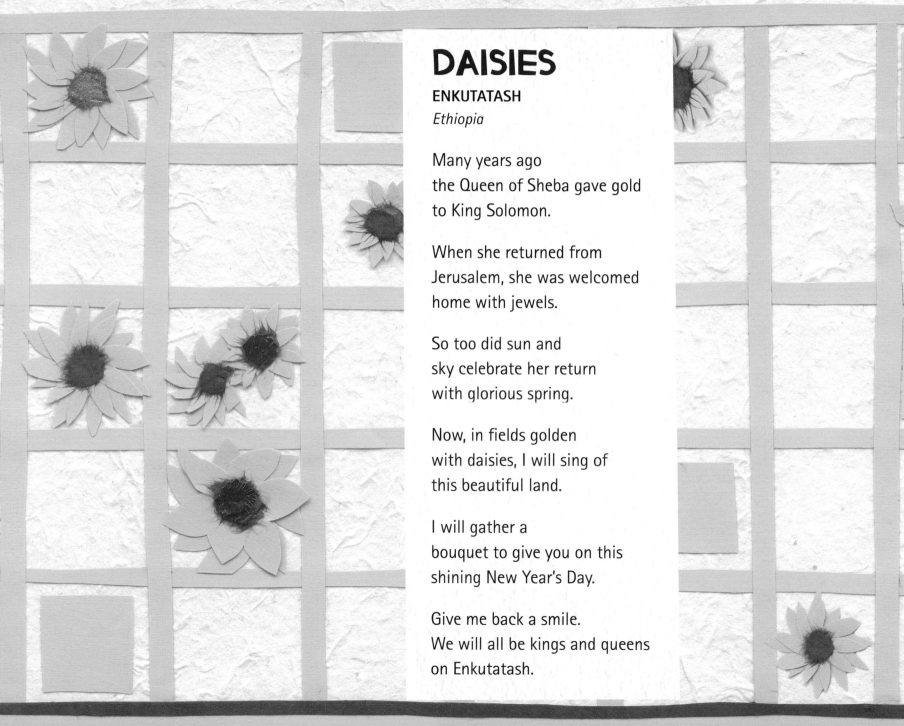

DAISIES

ENKUTATASH
Ethiopia

Many years ago
the Queen of Sheba gave gold
to King Solomon.

When she returned from
Jerusalem, she was welcomed
home with jewels.

So too did sun and
sky celebrate her return
with glorious spring.

Now, in fields golden
with daisies, I will sing of
this beautiful land.

I will gather a
bouquet to give you on this
shining New Year's Day.

Give me back a smile.
We will all be kings and queens
on Enkutatash.

CASTING AWAY SINS

ROSH HASHANAH
United States

This morning in the synagogue,
 we heard the shofar's loud, clear sound.
This evening in the house,
  we'll have apples dipped in honey,
   pomegranates with their ruby seeds.
But now, this sunny afternoon,
 we walk to the creek, our pockets full of bread.
"I'll tell you the truth. I lost the money,"
 my big sister whispers.
"I'll tell you the truth. I tore the dress,"
 I whisper back.
Then we toss the bread and our sins,
 and watch the flowing water carry them
  far, far away.

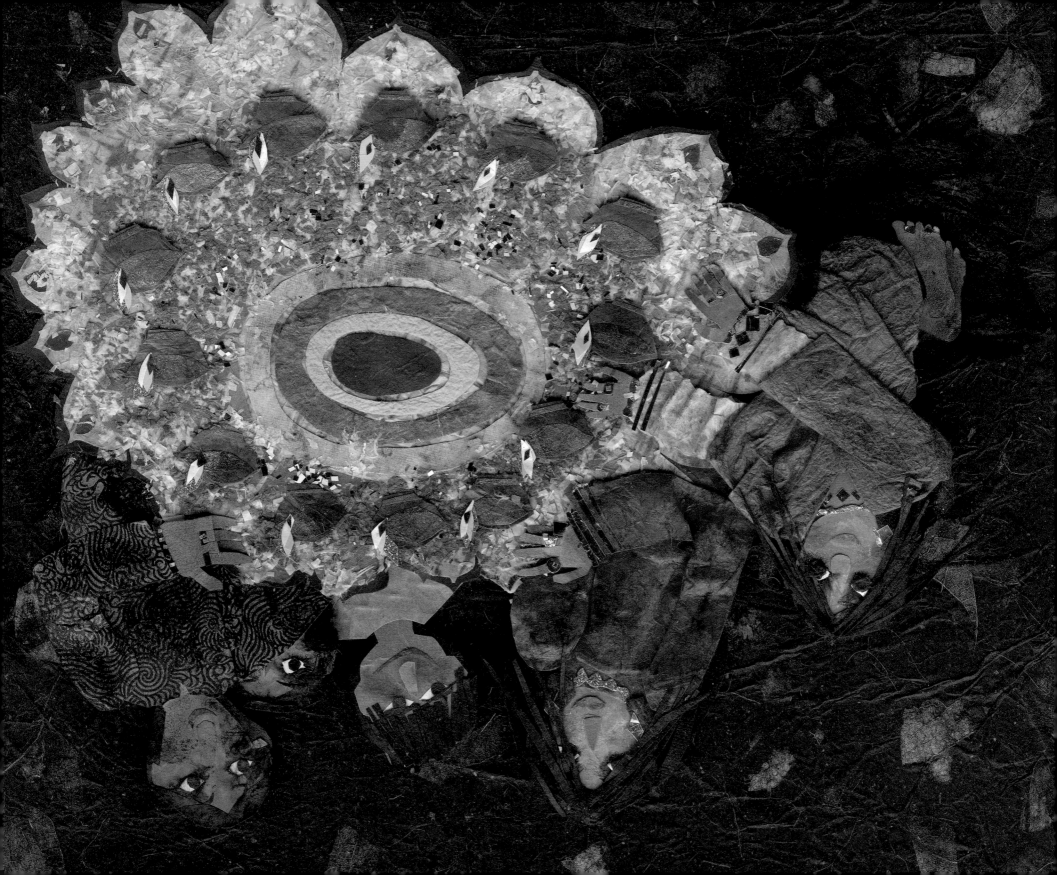

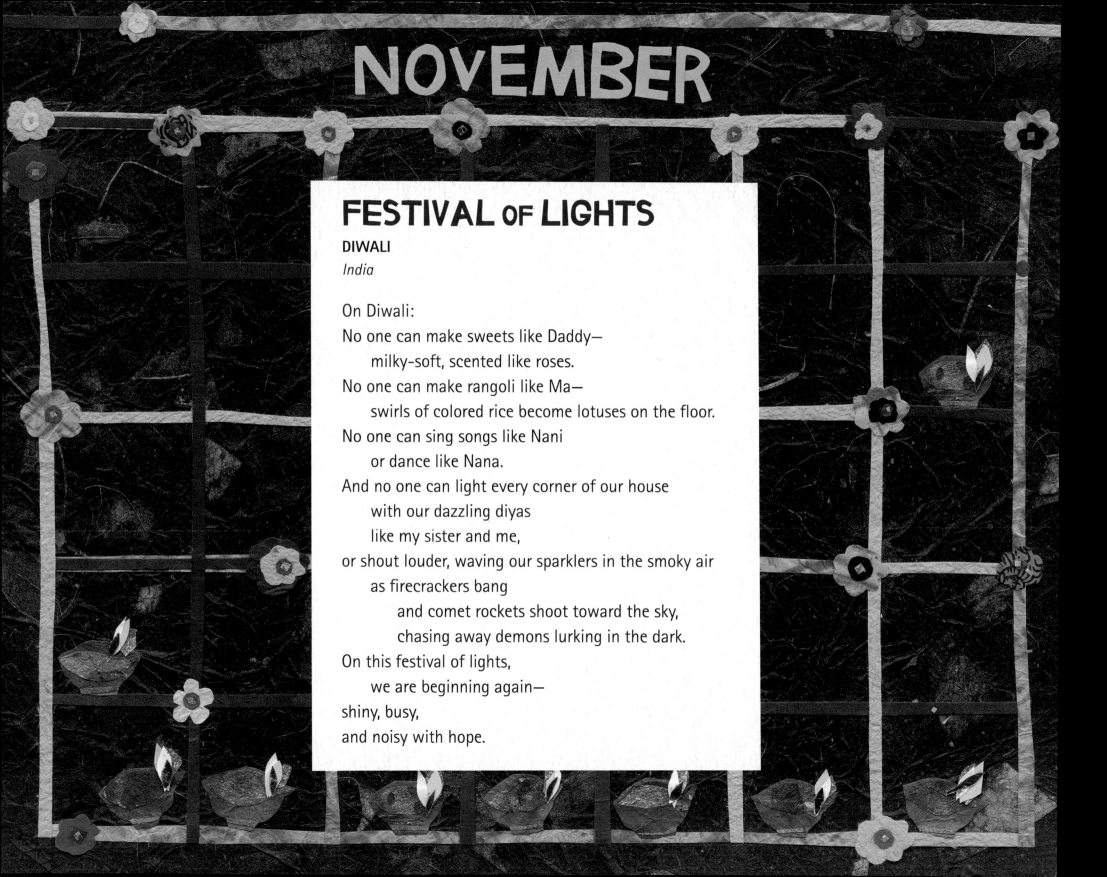

FESTIVAL OF LIGHTS

DIWALI
India

On Diwali:
No one can make sweets like Daddy—
    milky-soft, scented like roses.
No one can make rangoli like Ma—
    swirls of colored rice become lotuses on the floor.
No one can sing songs like Nani
    or dance like Nana.
And no one can light every corner of our house
    with our dazzling diyas
    like my sister and me,
or shout louder, waving our sparklers in the smoky air
    as firecrackers bang
      and comet rockets shoot toward the sky,
      chasing away demons lurking in the dark.
On this festival of lights,
    we are beginning again—
shiny, busy,
and noisy with hope.

FIRE IS BETTER

AÑO VIEJO
Ecuador

Some people say
    you can wash the bad away.
Yes, that may be true.
    But in my country, what we do
in the streets on this last of days
    is to set the bad ablaze.
We make gigantic effigies
    of cloth and sawdust, whatever we please,
with crazy masks of papier-mâché.
    Tonight they will burn in a brilliant display.
Papi, so brave, will jump over our fire.
    Mami won't let me till I can jump higher.
But I'll dance and cheer as the merry sparks fly.
    Año viejo, it's time for good-bye!

DECEMBER

LAS DOCE UVAS DE LA SUERTE

NOCHEVIEJA
Spain

Twelve grapes:
    twelve wishes on a plate.
Do not tempt fate.
Tonight, we stay up late.
And with each peal of the bell,
we eat, eat
    so each new month will be sweet.
May all our dreams come true.
¡Feliz Año Nuevo!
¡Buena suerte! to you.

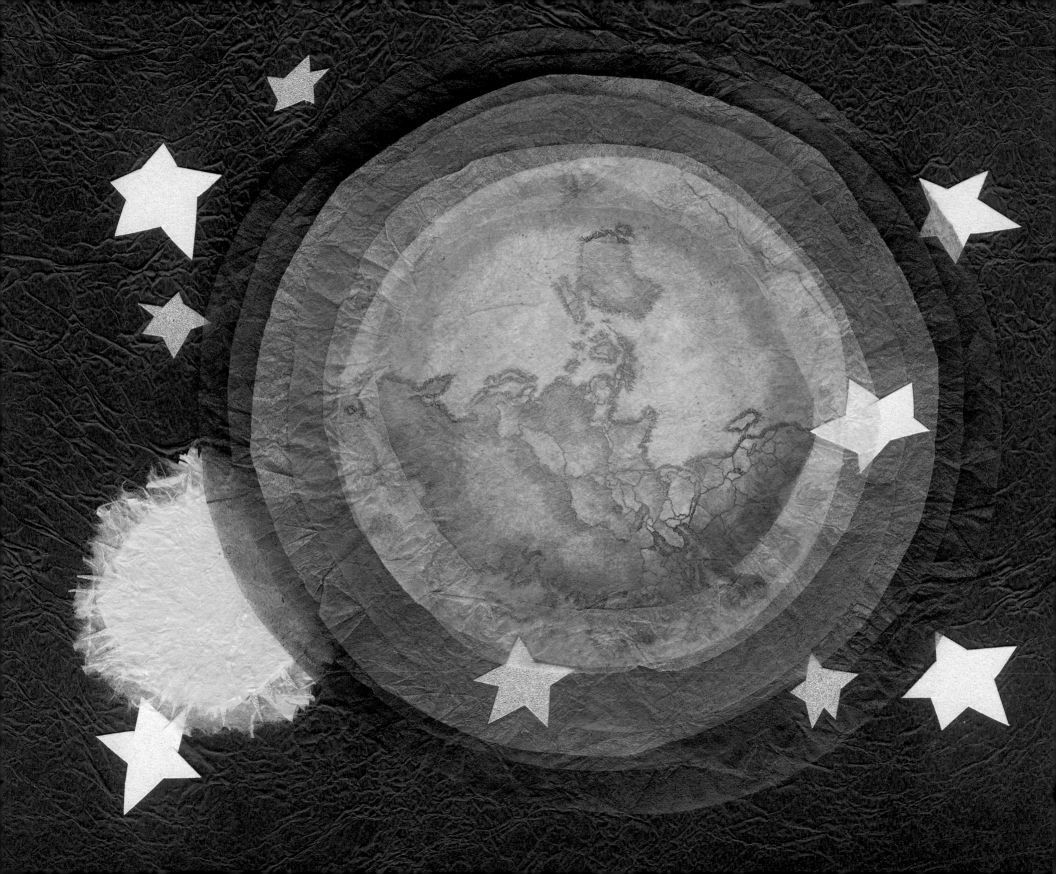

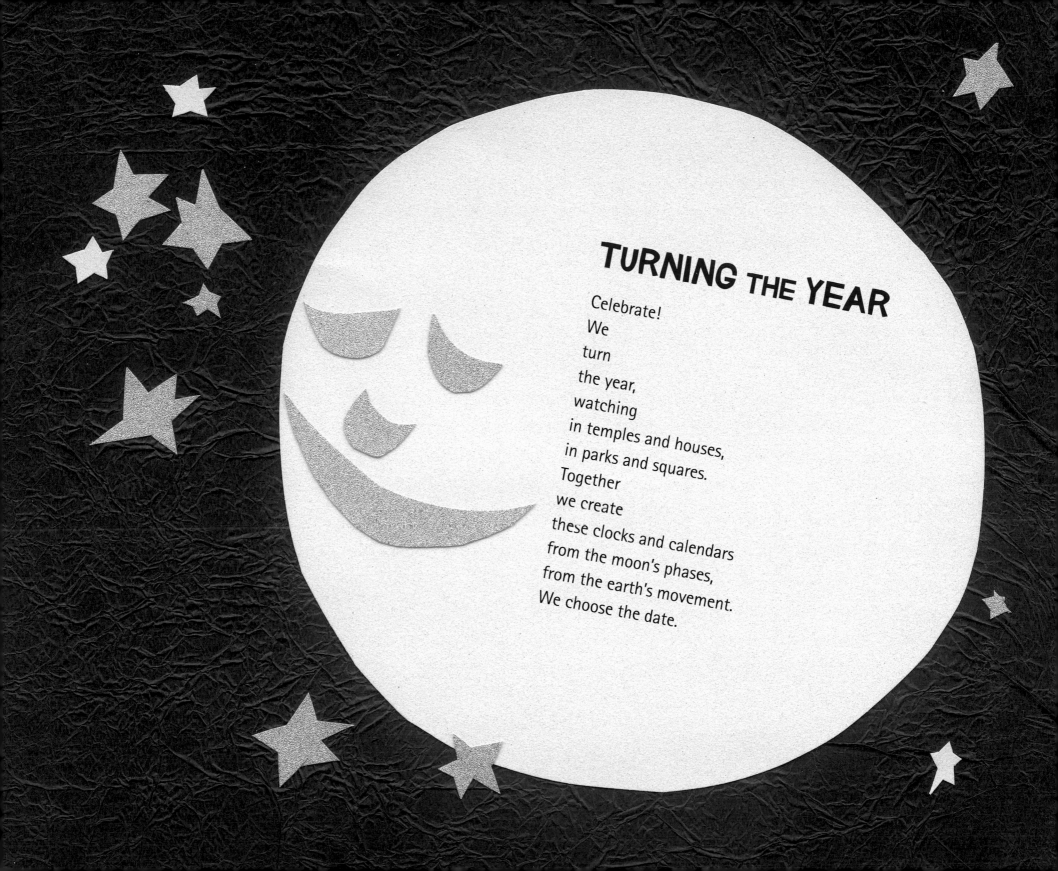

TURNING THE YEAR

Celebrate!
We
turn
the year,
watching
in temples and houses,
in parks and squares.
Together
we create
these clocks and calendars
from the moon's phases,
from the earth's movement.
We choose the date.

CALENDARS

For millennia, civilizations have marked the beginning of a new year with celebrations. The earliest recorded festivities date back four thousand years to the Babylonians, who celebrated the new year in March at the first new moon after the spring equinox in the Northern Hemisphere. Later civilizations developed and followed different calendars, so the date of New Year's Day depended on which calendar was being used.

New Year's Day was formally celebrated for the first time on January 1, 45 BCE, after the Roman emperor Julius Caesar introduced a solar calendar based on Earth's revolution around the sun. The calendar, which became known as the Julian calendar, consisted of 365 days and one leap (extra) day every four years, because it takes the earth approximately 365¼ days to revolve around the sun. The days were divided into twelve months of 30 or 31 days each. The month of January was named for Janus, the Roman god of gates and doors, beginnings and endings, whose two faces look backward and forward.

The Gregorian calendar, created in 1582 during the time of Pope Gregory XIII, corrected the mathematical formula used to calculate the leap year and inserted the extra day according to a different rule. A main reason for this reform was to prevent Easter Sunday from falling too far from the spring equinox in March. The Gregorian calendar is internationally the most common civil calendar in use today.

Other cultures and groups, such as Jews, Chinese, and Hindus, use a twelve-month lunar calendar, based on the cycle of the moon, to determine when the new year begins. These calendars generally add a thirteenth month every few years to align with the seasons. Although New Year's Day is on a different date each year, that date generally falls within the same few months for each group.

The Islamic calendar is a purely lunar calendar. It consists of 354 or 355 days and twelve months of 29 or 30 days. Each month begins when the new crescent moon is sighted, and those sightings vary from region to region due to cloud cover, sky brightness, and other factors. Because this calendar is shorter than the Gregorian calendar, the first month, Muharram, begins 10 or 11 days earlier than it did the previous year. This means that in some years, New Year's Day will be celebrated in May, as in this book.

NEW YEAR'S GREETINGS

The "Happy New Year" greetings below come from the languages spoken in the places represented in the poems. Spellings and pronunciations may vary, and some sounds cannot be reproduced exactly in English. The pronunciations provided are the best approximations for English speakers in the United States.

English (United States): Happy New Year (HAP-ee noo yeer)

Scots (Scotland): A Guid New Year (a gid noo yeer) *or* Happy Hogmanay (HAP-ee HOG-muh-nay *or* HOG-muh-NAY)

Russian (Russia): S Novym Godom (sNO-vym GO-dom)

Chinese (China): Mandarin: Gong xi fa cai (goong sse fah tsai); Cantonese: Gong hey fat choy (gung hey fat choi). Wishing you joy and prosperity for the new year.

Persian (Iran): Sale No Mobarak (SAHL-eh noh moh-BAH-rak) *or* Nowruz Mobarak (noh-ROOZ moh-BAH-rak)

Thai (Thailand): males say: Sawasdee Pii Mai Krab (sa-WAH-dee pee my krahb); females say: Sawasdee Pii Mai Ka (sa-WAH-dee pee my kah)

Arabic (Jordan): Sana Sa'eedah (SAH-nah sah-EE-dah) *or* Kul'aam wa antum bikhayr (KOOL-ahm wah AN-tum bi-KHAIR). May you be well throughout the year.

Māori (New Zealand): Ngā mihi o te Tau Hou (nah mee-hee oh teh TAU hoh)

Mapuche (Chile): Auki we tripantu (AW-kee weh tree-pan-TOO). The new year has come. *Also* Wiñoi tripantu (wee-NYOI tree-pan-TOO). The sunrise has returned.

Kemetic (United States, Ancient Egypt): Di Wep Ronpet Nofret (dee wep RON-pet NOH-fret)

Gujarati (India): Sal Mubarak (sahl moo-BAH-rak) *or* Navroze Mubarak (nav-ROHS moo-BAH-rak)

Amharic (Ethiopia): Melkam Addis Amet (mel-KAM ahd-DIS ah-MET)

Hebrew (United States): L'shanah tovah (le-shah-NAH toh-VAH). May you have a good year.

Hindi (India): Naya Saal Mubarak (nuh-YAH sahl moo-BAH-ruck); greeting combines Hindi and Urdu words

Spanish (Ecuador, Spain): Feliz Año Nuevo (feh-LEEZ AN-yoh NOOWAY-voh)

ABOUT THE CELEBRATIONS

MIDNIGHT BALL DROP
December 31: NEW YEAR'S EVE
New York City, United States

The Times Square ball drop is one of the most famous New Year's Eve festivities. About a million people gather in New York City each year to witness the Waterford crystal–covered ball descend a pole atop a building, One Times Square, and more than a billion people worldwide watch the event via satellite.

The first New Year's Eve celebration in Times Square was held on December 31, 1904, to commemorate the opening of the Times Tower, the new headquarters of the *New York Times*. The event was orchestrated by Adolph Ochs, owner of the newspaper, and it featured fireworks displays. When the city banned fireworks a few years later, Ochs commissioned the original seven-hundred-pound ball to be made and lowered from the tower flagpole, starting at 11:59 pm and coming to a stop at exactly midnight. Since then the ball has dropped every year except 1942 and 1943, when the United States was engaged in World War II. Today the *New York Times* headquarters are in a different location, but the ball drop is still held in Times Square. Besides the ball drop, the celebration once again features fireworks, as well as live musical performances and more than a ton of confetti!

FIRST FOOTING
December 31–January 1: HOGMANAY
Scotland

Hogmanay is the last day of the old year and the first day of the new one. There are many customs associated with this Scottish festival. A thorough housecleaning is one tradition. Another is singing "Auld Lang Syne," a song based on a poem by the Scottish poet Robert Burns, at "the bells" (midnight). Some Scottish communities also hold fire ceremonies—torchlight processions, bonfires, fireworks, or the swinging of huge fireballs made of lit rags, papers, sticks, and other materials—to symbolize the power of the sun and to drive away evil forces.

Then there is the ritual of First Footing, the arrival of the first person to enter one's home after midnight. For good luck and abundance, the First Footer is supposed to bring whiskey and a type of fruitcake or

shortbread, as well as coal for the fireplace and sometimes coins for prosperity and salt to flavor a meal. According to tradition, the most welcome First Footer is a tall, dark-haired man. This may be because Scotland was once conquered by Vikings, who often had red or blond hair. So to the Scots, light-haired men meant trouble. Today, people welcome men and women of all types as First Footers. In exchange for the First Footer's gifts, the host offers food and drink. Then more guests may arrive, and the party goes into full swing, sometimes well into New Year's Day. It's traditional for family and friends to have lunch or dinner together on January 1, and the usual fare is steak pie.

TWO NEW YEARS
December 31–January 1 and January 13–14: RUSSIAN NEW YEARS
Russia

To calculate holidays, the Russian Orthodox Church uses the Julian calendar. According to this calendar, Christmas falls on January 7 and New Year's Day on January 14. From 1917 to 1992, the Soviet government banned religious celebrations such as Christmas and accompanying traditions such as a Christmas tree. Instead, Russian people decorated trees for the secular New Year, with January 1 being "New" New Year's Day. They told their children that on "New" New Year's Eve, Grandfather Frost (Ded Moroz) and his granddaughter, Snow Maiden (Snegurochka), would come by troika, a sleigh pulled by three horses, to deliver gifts.

Today, Russians once again observe Christmas on January 7, *after* "New" New Year's Day, which is a big public holiday. The festivities include parties, presents, and fireworks. But many people in the former Soviet Union nations, including Russia and other Eastern European countries, also celebrate Stary Novy God, "Old" New Year, two weeks later, on January 14. The decorated trees remain standing through "Old" New Year's Day; and families celebrate with large meals, carols, and some friendly fortune-telling.

DRAGON DANCE
February: CHINESE NEW YEAR
Hong Kong, China

Chinese New Year, or Spring Festival, which falls sometime in January or February according to the lunar calendar, is one of the most

(continued on next page)

important, and most likely the oldest, of all Chinese holidays. It is celebrated throughout Asia and in Asian communities around the world. Chinese New Year originally marked the start of the agricultural year and honored gods and ancestors. Today, as in the past, it is a time to gather with friends and family and celebrate with feasting and gift giving. People hand out money in red envelopes because red is the color of happiness and good fortune. Other festivities associated with the holiday include spring-cleaning, decorating houses with scrolls and lanterns, and lighting fireworks and firecrackers, although they are now banned in many places for safety reasons.

Each year of the Chinese calendar is associated with one of twelve animals. One of those animals is a dragon. It is thought to be a good-luck creature that symbolizes power, wisdom, and long life. At Chinese New Year celebrations, the Dragon Dance is performed to scare away demons and bring life-giving rain.

A dancing dragon may be made of fabric, wood, metal, and/or plastic; and it varies in size and length. Its color is symbolic. For example, a green dragon stands for a good harvest, a red one for excitement. Coordinating their movements to the beat of a drum, dancers work as a team to manipulate the dragon, imitating the creature's rippling motion and bringing it to life. The dragon's performance is the highlight of many Chinese New Year festivities, for both dancers and spectators alike.

THIRTEEN DAYS
March: NOWRUZ

Iran

Nowruz (one of various spellings for this holiday in English), from the Persian words for "new" and "day," is a festival that takes place for thirteen days, beginning on the spring equinox, to celebrate the new year. The holiday originated in Persia (modern-day Iran). Nowruz is a secular holiday that today is celebrated and revered worldwide by people of different religions and cultures.

To prepare for Nowruz, families clean their homes, buy new clothes, cook special foods, and sprout wheat, barley, bean, or lentil seeds that will be put on the *haft seen* table. *Haft* is the Persian word for "seven," and *seen* is the word for the letter *s*. A haft seen table features seven symbolic items with names that start with the letter *s*: *somaq* (sumac, a spice that gives life flavor); *senjed* (dried fruit of a lotus tree, to represent love); *serkeh* (vinegar, for patience and age); *seeb* (apple, for health and beauty); *seer* (garlic, also for health); *samanu* (wheat

pudding, for prosperity); and *sabzeh* (the sprouted seeds that stand for rebirth). In addition to these items, the haft seen table may also hold other symbolic objects such as hyacinth flowers, coins, eggs, candles, holy books and/or poetry books, a mirror for reflection on the past year, and a bowl of goldfish to represent new life.

During the holiday, people gather with friends and relatives and go on outings. On the thirteenth and last day, families picnic in a park or other outdoor area and throw away the sabzeh, which they believe has collected all the negativity in the house. Young single people sometimes tie knots in the sabzeh before tossing it into a river or stream while wishing for a companion. For everyone, Nowruz is a time of hope. A new day, a new year has begun!

WASHING THE BAD AWAY
April: SONGKRAN

Thailand

Songkran, the Thai New Year celebration, is observed from April 13 to 15, at the end of the dry season. It is also celebrated in other Southeast Asian countries, including Laos, Cambodia, and Myanmar. The festival begins with housecleaning and paying homage to Buddha by cleansing statues and washing the hands of monks, parents, and other respected elders. People build stupas—towers of sand—and adorn them with flags, flowers, and other decorations. Because Buddhists carry out sand from the floor on their feet or shoes when they leave their temples, they view the stupas as a way of returning that sand to the temples. For Buddhists, all these actions are ways of "making merit," of doing good deeds that will earn happiness and the wisdom to know what true happiness is, leading to the highest wisdom: enlightenment.

Songkran is also marked by feasts and colorful processions. But perhaps the most famous part of the festival is the water throwing, a symbolic way to wash away bad thoughts and the past year's misfortune and get a fresh start for the new year. People of all ages gather in the streets, some riding in pickup trucks and other vehicles, with buckets of water, water guns, and hoses, ready to splash and spray any friends or strangers they encounter. In some areas, even elephants line the streets and squirt water on passersby. Festivalgoers will also sometimes dab their faces with a soothing paste made from talcum powder and water to ward off evil. Because Songkran falls during the hottest time of the year in Thailand, the cool water is a blessing in more ways than one.

NEW MOON, NEW YEAR

May: FIRST DAY OF MUHARRAM

Jordan

The Islamic New Year occurs on the first day of Muharram, which is the first month of the Islamic calendar. Muharram is considered one of the four sacred months of the year. The first Muslim year is counted from Prophet Muhammad's ﷺ *Hijra* in 622 CE. This was the time of his emigration on the Arabian Peninsula from Mecca, where there was a plot to kill him, to Medina, where he was welcomed. In Medina, Prophet Muhammad ﷺ built the first *masjid*, or mosque, and established the first Muslim community. On the first day of Muharram, Muslims reflect on these occurrences and on their own lives and deeds, and perhaps make new year's resolutions. People also commemorate the death of Prophet Muhammad's ﷺ grandson and his followers at the battle of Karbalā on the tenth day of Muharram in 680 CE, as well as the liberation of the Israelites from Egypt.

The Islamic New Year is welcomed in a number of ways by different groups. For many people, it is a time of prayer, reflection, and charity. Some also fast on certain days during the month, although the fasts are not required. Children are often told the story of Prophet Muhammad's ﷺ Hijra at home until they are old enough to sit still and welcome the new year in the mosque.

BRINGING TOGETHER EARTH AND SKY

June: MATARIKI

New Zealand

In the Māori language, the star cluster known to astronomers as the Pleiades, or the Seven Sisters, is called Matariki, which has two meanings: "little eyes" and "eyes of god." A Māori legend says that the God of the Winds became so angry at his brothers for separating their parents, the God of the Sky and the Goddess of the Earth, that he tore out his eyes and flung them into the heavens, where they became stars. Another Māori story says that Matariki is a mother, surrounded by her six daughters. The stars reappear in the sky in June, which is when winter begins in New Zealand and other Southern Hemisphere countries, to revive the sun, tired from its long journey. When the star cluster Matariki appears just before sunrise, the new year begins.

Traditionally this is a time to harvest the last of the year's crops and prepare the ground for the coming year. It is also an opportunity for Māori to focus on *whakapapa*, their ancestry, and the links among and

respect for all living things since the beginning of time. During the festivities, children and adults fly kites as a way to communicate with gods and goddesses and to bring together family and friends, and Earth and sky. These celebrations dwindled in the mid-twentieth century but were revived in the twenty-first century. Today, Matariki unites all New Zealanders as well as other people throughout the South Pacific.

THE YOUNG SUN RISES

June: WE TRIPANTU

Chile

In late June, the Mapuche people in Chile and Argentina celebrate We Tripantu, the return of the sun after the shortest day of the year in the Southern Hemisphere. Festivities begin on the winter solstice, with ceremonies traditionally led by a *machi*, a spiritual guide, who directs people to thank nature and the universe and to ask for prosperity in the coming year. The ceremonies are usually held near a *rewe* (or *rehue*), a tree trunk carved with steps that is set in the ground and often decorated with branches from the sacred *foye* (canelo) tree. The rewe represents the tree of life and serves as an altar. Also known as the machi's ladder, the rewe allows the machi to communicate with the spiritual world.

On the evening of June 23, families, friends, and neighbors gather to feast, tell stories, and play music throughout the night on instruments such as the *trutruca* (horn), the *pifilca* (flute), and the *cultrún* (drum). At dawn, people go outside to welcome the young sun with the greeting "Wiñoi Tripantu!" Then they head to rivers and other bodies of water to cleanse themselves of all negativity from the old year and restore themselves for the year to come. Throughout the day, people play games and dance, circling the rewe (or sometimes a foye tree) in celebration of nature's rebirth.

SMASHING THE POTS

July: WEP RONPET

United States/Ancient Egypt

The Egyptians were among the first ancient people to calculate time. Originally they did so based on their knowledge of the stars. In Kemet, ancient Egypt, during the season of Akhet, the new year was celebrated sometime between mid-July and early August when Sopdet (also known as Sirius, the Dog Star) rose before sunrise. This was an important time of year. People were filled with hope that the river Nile would be flooded

(continued on next page)

with just the right amount of water so that crops would flourish in the next growing season. They celebrated with gatherings and feasts.

Today some people still practice a religion based on traditional Kemetic spiritual beliefs. The main temple of one of the most popular branches of this religion is located in Joliet, Illinois, in the United States. On Wep Ronpet, or "Opening the Year," followers purify themselves and their homes. They set up shrines to particular gods and present them with offerings of food and drink. People also perform the practice of execration, the destruction of injustices, bad habits, or other things that have blocked personal growth in the past year. One method of execration is to write these things on red clay pots and then smash (or bury or otherwise demolish) the pots. This clears the way for a bright and promising new year.

NOWRUZ, NAVROZE
August: NAVROZE
India
The name for the Persian New Year has different spellings and pronunciations throughout the world. One typical English spelling for the holiday observed by the Parsi community is Navroze.

The Parsis are followers of the Persian prophet Zoroaster (or Zarathustra), who lived centuries ago. They emigrated from Persia (modern-day Iran) to India, bringing along their faith and customs. They believe in one God, Ahura Mazdā, represented in their temples by sacred eternal fires scented with offerings of sandalwood incense. Parsis also keep a smaller fire burning in their homes. While Iranians and other people celebrate Nowruz in the spring, Parsis, who use a different calendar, celebrate Navroze in August, although some people observe the holiday both times of the year.

The last day of the year is known as Pateti. It is a quiet day for reflection, righting wrongs, and repenting past sins. Then comes Navroze, New Year's Day. Parsis begin the day by visiting the *agiary*, fire temple. Then they pay respects to their elders and welcome family and friends to their homes, greeting them with "Navroze Mubarak!" Houses are decorated with flowers and *chawk*, decorative patterns made from colored powder. Feasting is a major part of the holiday, with dishes such as *pulao* (a rice dish), *patra ni machi* (fish in banana leaves), dal (lentils cooked with ghee, clarified butter), and many sweets. Afterward, people may go to a play or another cultural event. Navroze is a day to celebrate the Parsis' unique identity, as well as the things all people have in common.

DAISIES
September: ENKUTATASH
Ethiopia
The ancient Ethiopian, or Nile, calendar was first based on the stars, then on the solar year. By 238 BCE, the calendar consisted of twelve months, each thirty days long, plus a "small month" of five days, with a sixth day added every four years. This became the Ethiopic calendar, and it is still in use in Ethiopia today.

Enkutatash, Ethiopian New Year, on the Ethiopic calendar corresponds to September 11 on the Gregorian calendar. Enkutatash is believed to be the day the Queen of Sheba returned to her homeland after her visit to King Solomon in Jerusalem in 980 BCE. She was welcomed with *enku*, jewels. Enkutatash, which means "gift of jewels," has another ancient meaning that commemorates the receding of the great flood during the time of Noah. The day also marks the end of the rainy season and the beginning of sunny days.

Today, on Enkutatash, children in new, white, hand-woven cotton clothes offer yellow Meskel daisies, along with pictures they have painted, as gifts to friends and neighbors. In return, the youngsters are given money or small gifts. People also celebrate by going to church, eating a traditional meal of *doro wot* (chicken stew) and injera (flat bread), sharing coffee, and singing and dancing. Some may send greeting cards wishing one another "Melkam Addis Amet!" Happy New Year to You!

CASTING AWAY SINS
October: ROSH HASHANAH
United States
In September or October, Jews all over the world celebrate Rosh Hashanah, the Jewish New Year. In synagogues, the holiday is announced by the blowing of the shofar, a ram's horn. This begins the High Holy Days, also known as the Days of Awe or the Ten Days of Repentance, which end with Yom Kippur, the Day of Atonement. During this time, God decides the fates of the good and the wicked and those who fall somewhere in between. Everyone has until Yom Kippur to repent for any wrongs committed during the past year.

During the two days Rosh Hashanah is observed, people go to the synagogue to pray, and eat special foods, including apples dipped in honey for a sweet year and pomegranates for fruitfulness. Some Jews, wherever they live, also practice *tashlich*, the casting away of sins. The sins are symbolized by bits of bread or stones, which are tossed into a body of water, such as a river, a lake, or the ocean. Another custom during the High Holy Days is to apologize directly to the individuals whom one has wronged. This is a time to recognize one's mistakes and to resolve not to make them again in the new year.

FESTIVAL OF LIGHTS
November: DIWALI
India

Celebrated in October or November, Diwali, the Hindu Festival of Lights, coincides with the new moon during the month of Kartik on the lunar calendar. Lasting for five days, Diwali represents the triumph of good over evil and light over darkness. It began as a harvest festival as well as the period when people closed out their accounts and prayed for success in the coming year. Today Diwali still marks the end of the financial year and is a time for taking stock of past behavior and hoping to do better. In many parts of India, it is viewed as the start of the new year and an opportunity to strengthen family ties and social relationships.

Various legends and beliefs are associated with the holiday. On Diwali, in some regions of India (and in other countries), people honor Lakshmi, goddess of wealth and prosperity. West Bengalis in eastern India pay tribute to Kali, goddess of time and change. In some southern states, Diwali is celebrated to honor the god Krishna's victory over the demon king Narakasura. In northern India, the holiday celebrates the story of the prince Lord Rama, who left home to live in the forest for fourteen years; fought demons to rescue his wife, Sita; and then returned to his kingdom, to jubilant greetings.

To celebrate Diwali, people clean their homes and decorate them with *rangoli*, designs made from colored rice, flour, sand, and/or flower petals. They make offerings and prayers to the gods and goddesses. They light *diyas* (or *divas*), clay lamps, and leave open their doors and windows to invite Lakshmi into their homes. To chase away evil spirits, people set off firecrackers and fireworks. With friends and family, they feast and exchange sweets and gifts. Diwali is one of the biggest of all Indian holidays, and the most joyous.

FIRE IS BETTER
December 31: AÑO VIEJO
Ecuador

For the new year, people of all cultures focus on getting rid of negativity from the past year. Some use water to cleanse or float away failures, regrets, and mistakes. Ecuadorians use fire. They burn away the Año Viejo, old year, by making or buying *monigotes* (also called *años viejos*), dummies with masks, and setting them ablaze at midnight. The monigotes represent all kinds of figures, ranging from popular celebrities to disliked ones, from politicians to cartoon characters, and from cultural icons to relatives and other individuals. The dummies come in all sizes and are made of cloth stuffed with materials that burn quickly, such as newspaper, sawdust, or small cardboard pieces. Most masks are made of papier-mâché.

Some towns and organizations hold competitions for the best monigotes. As the dummies burn, revelers jump over the flames twelve times for good luck in the new year. The "death" of the dummies leaves *viudas* ("widows"), usually men and teenage boys dressed festively as women, who stop people and traffic on the streets and entertain for money.

The custom of burning monigotes may have begun tragically during a yellow fever epidemic in Ecuador in 1895. Coffins filled with the clothes and other effects of the dead were burned to disinfect the homes. But gradually the custom became a broader and more symbolic way to get rid of the bad and welcome the good.

LAS DOCE UVAS DE LA SUERTE
December 31: NEW YEAR'S EVE
Spain

As clocks all across Spain chime midnight on Nochevieja, December 31, Spaniards celebrate by eating twelve grapes in twelve seconds, one grape at each peal of the bell. The grapes are said to bring good luck for the twelve months ahead and perhaps grant wishes, especially if the grapes are sweet. For the charm to work, all the grapes are supposed to be chewed and swallowed by the last peal of the bell—not an easy feat!

No one is exactly sure how the tradition began. Some stories say it became popular in Madrid in the late 1800s when people gathered in a public square at midnight to hear the bells chime and to mock the way wealthy upper-class people celebrated the new year with grapes and champagne. Others believe the custom was started in 1909 by grape growers who wanted to sell more of their fruit. Today, eating twelve lucky grapes is also popular in Mexico and other Latin American countries, in the Philippines, and in parts of the United States. Even if trying to eat all those grapes in twelve seconds does not make wishes come true, it usually brings laughter, which is a very good way to start the new year.

GLOSSARY AND PRONUNCIATION GUIDE

Pronunciations of the non-English words and terms that follow may vary, and some sounds cannot be reproduced exactly in English. The pronunciations provided approximate the way the words and terms are spoken by English speakers in the United States.

agiary (AH-jer-ee): fire temple; Zoroastrian house of worship in which fire is always kept burning

Ahura Mazdā (ah-HOO-rah MAZ-dah): deity recognized as the supreme God of the universe in the Zoroastrian religion; the name means "Wise Lord"

Akhet (AH-ket): first of three ancient Egyptian seasons

Año Viejo (AN-yoh vee-AY-hoh): old year; also a term for an effigy, or a stuffed doll (*monigote*)

"Auld Lang Syne" (ohld lang sahyn): Scottish song traditionally sung at midnight on New Year's Eve; *auld lang syne* means "days gone by" or "old times"

babushka (BAH-boosh-kuh): grandmother or elderly woman

Buddha (BOO-duh): Indian religious leader whose teachings about the way to enlightenment were the basis for Buddhism; also used to refer to a statue or picture representing Buddha

buena suerte (BWAY-nah SWEAR-tay): good luck

chawk (chawk): decorative pattern in Parsi home made from colored powder; also spelled "chowk"

cultrún (cool-TROON): large, wooden drum used by the Mapuche

dal (dahl): lentils, beans, or peas cooked with spices in clarified butter (ghee)

Ded Moroz (dyed mah-ROS): Grandfather Frost; mythical Slavic character who brings gifts to children on New Year's Eve

Diwali (dih-VAH-lee): five-day Festival of Lights that coincides with the Hindu New Year

diya (DEE-yuh): small oil lamp made of clay; also called a *diva* (DEE-vuh)

doro wot (DOOR-oh what): Ethiopian stew made with chicken and spices

effigy (EF-i-jee): stuffed doll made to look like a popular or disliked person or figure

enku (en-KOO): jewels

Enkutatash (en-KOO-tah-TASCH): Ethiopian New Year

equinox (EE-kwuh-nocks): time in spring and fall when there are the same number of hours of darkness and light all around the world

execration (ek-si-KREY-shuhn): act of declaring something to be wrong or evil

foye (foi): sacred canelo tree of the Mapuche

ghee (gee): clarified butter; melted butter from which the fat has been skimmed off

haft seen (HAHFT seen): holiday table containing seven special dishes of food with names that start with the letter *s* in Persian

Hijra (HIJ-ruh *or* HIDJ-ruh): flight of Prophet Muhammad☪ from Mecca to Medina in 622 CE

Hogmanay (HOG-muh-nay *or* HOG-muh-NAY): New Year's Eve/New Year's Day celebration in Scotland

injera (in-JER-ah): spongy flatbread made of fermented flour; used to scoop up meat and vegetable stews

Jerusalem (je-ROO-suh-luhm): holy city in the Middle East sacred to Jews, Christians, and Muslims

Kali (KAH-lee): Hindu goddess seen as the destroyer of evil, mother of the universe, and a representative of feminine energy

Karbalā (KAHR-bah-lah): holy city of Islam, located in central Iraq; site of a battle in which Prophet Muhammad's☪ grandson was killed on the tenth day of Muharram, 680 CE

Kartik (kahr-TIK): eighth month of the Hindu lunar calendar

Kemet (KEH-met): ancient Egypt

King Solomon (king SOL-uh-muhn): ancient king of Israel famous for his wisdom

Krishna (KRISH-nuh): eighth incarnation of the Hindu god Vishnu; Krishna represents love, compassion, and playfulness, and is known for his bravery in destroying evil

Lakshmi (LUHK-shmee *or* LAK-shmee): Hindu goddess of wealth and prosperity

las doce uvas de la suerte (lahs DOH-seh OO-vahs deh lah SWEAR-tay): the twelve lucky grapes

Little Eyes (LIT-uhl eyez): Māori name for the star cluster Matariki; also known as Pleiades, or the Seven Sisters

machi (MAH-chee): traditional Mapuche spiritual guide and healer

Mami (MAH-mee): Spanish for "Mom"

Māori (MAU-ree *or* MAH-ree): Polynesian people native to New Zealand

Mapuche (mah-POOCH-ay *or* muh-PUSCH): one of the groups of people native to Chile and Argentina

masjid (MAHS-jid): mosque; Muslim place of worship

Matariki (mah-tahr-EE-kee): Māori name for the star cluster also known as Pleiades, or the Seven Sisters; when Matariki rises in the Southern Hemisphere winter sky, it signifies the start of a new year

Mecca (MEK-uh): most important holy city of Islam, located in western Saudi Arabia; birthplace of Prophet Muhammad☪

Medina (muh-DEE-nuh): second most important holy city of Islam, located in western Saudi Arabia; site of the first mosque and the tomb of Prophet Muhammad☪

millennia (mi-LEN-ee-uh): thousands of years

monigote (MOH-nee-GOH-tay): stuffed doll or dummy with a papier-mâché head or mask

Muhammad☪ (moo-HAM-id *or* moo-HAH-muhd): Arab prophet who was the founder of Islam

Muharram (moo-HARR-um): first month of the Islamic year and one of four sacred months of the Islamic calendar

Nana (NAH-nah): Hindi term for maternal grandfather

Nani (NAH-nee): Hindi term for maternal grandmother

Narakasura (NAH-rah-KAH-soo-rah): demon king in Hindu mythology

Navroze (nav-ROHS): Parsi New Year's Day

Nile (nahyl): river in northeastern Africa; considered to be the longest river in the world

Nochevieja (NOH-chay-vee-AY-hah): old night; New Year's Eve in Spanish-speaking countries

Nowruz (noh-ROOZ): Iranian spring festival that begins the new year

Papi (PAH-pee): Spanish for "Dad"

papier-mâché (PAY-pur muh-SHAY or PAP-yay mash-AY): paper mixed with glue and water that can be molded into desired shapes and that becomes hard when dry

Parsi (PAHR-see): person originally from India or Pakistan who follows the religion of Zoroastrianism

Pateti (peh-TEH-tee): Parsi New Year's Eve (last day of the year)

patra ni machi (PAH-tra ni mah-CHEE): Parsi dish of fish coated with herbs and spices, wrapped in banana leaves, and steamed

Persia (PUR-shuh): vast historic region in southwest Asia in the area now known as Iran

pifilca (pee-FEEL-kah): type of flute used by the Mapuche

Pleiades (PLEE-uh-deez): star cluster in the constellation Taurus; also known as the Seven Sisters

pulao (PULL-ow): rice dish containing vegetables and/or meat cooked in seasoned broth

Queen of Sheba (kween ov SHEE-buh): woman of power and seeker of truth and wisdom who appears in religious texts sacred to Muslims, Christians, and Jews

Rama (RAH-muh): seventh incarnation of the Hindu god Vishnu; Rama is known for his chivalry and righteousness

rangoli (run-GOH-lee): traditional design created on the floor using colored rice, sand, flower petals, or other materials

rewe (REE-way): sacred altar made from a tree trunk carved with seven steps; also called a *rehue* (REE-way)

Rosh Hashanah (ROHSH hah-SHAH-nuh or ROHSH hah-shah-NAH): Jewish New Year; holiday that begins the High Holy Days

sabzeh (SAHB-sey): lentil, wheat, bean, or barley sprouts

samanu (sah-MAHN-oo): sweet pudding or paste made from wheat

secular (SEK-yuh-ler): not religious; of or relating to things in the physical world and not to spiritual things

seeb (seeb): apple

seer (seer): garlic

senjed (sen-JED): dried fruit of a lotus tree

serkeh (ser-KEH): vinegar

shofar (shoh-FAHR): ram's horn trumpet blown during the Jewish High Holy Days

Sirius (SIR-ee-uhs): brightest star visible from any part of Earth, found in the constellation Canis Major; also known as the Dog Star

Sita (SEE-tah): incarnation of the Hindu goddess Lakshmi and wife of the Hindu god Rama; Sita represents devotion and virtue

Snegurochka (snee-GOO-rach-kah): Snow Maiden; character from Russian folktales considered to be the granddaughter of Ded Moroz; she accompanies him on New Year's Eve to deliver gifts

solstice (SOHL-stiss): time in summer and winter when the sun is farthest north or south of the equator

somaq (soh-MOK): sumac; used as a spice when the fruit is dried and powered

Songkran (song-GRAAN): water festival that marks the beginning of the Thai new year

Sopdet (SAHP-det): ancient Egyptian name for Sirius, the Dog Star

Soviet Union (SOH-vee-et YOON-yuhn): Union of Soviet Socialist Republics; former union of fifteen countries, including Russia, in eastern Europe and northern and western Asia

Stary Novy God (STA-riy NO-viy gohd): Russian "Old" New Year

stupa (STOO-puh): dome- or pyramid-shaped structure built of sand, dirt, or other materials, to honor Buddha or to commemorate an event or a sacred spot

synagogue (SIN-a-gog) Jewish place of worship

tashlich (tahsh-LEEKH or TAHSH-likh): Jewish practice in which sins are symbolically cast off into a body of water

troika (TROI-kuh): sleigh, carriage, or wagon pulled by three horses side by side

trutruca (true-TRUE-kah): long, coiled, trumpetlike horn used by the Mapuche

viuda (VYOO-dah): widow

Wep Ronpet (WHEP rahn-PET): Kemetic New Year; marked by the rising of Sopdet (Sirius)

West Bengali (west ben-GAH-lee): person who lives in West Bengal, a state in eastern India

We Tripantu (weh tree-pan-TOO): Mapuche New Year; takes place on the winter solstice in the Southern Hemisphere

whakapapa (FAHK-a-PAH-pah): Māori concept of ancestry or genealogy

Zoroaster (zor-oh-ASS-tur): ancient prophet from Persia who is regarded as the founder of the religious system Zoroastrianism; also known as Zarathustra (zah-ruh-THOO-struh)

AUTHOR'S SOURCES

In addition to consulting with people from or knowledgeable about the cultures and countries represented in the book as detailed in the acknowledgments, the following sources were used, all current as of the book's publication date.

HISTORY OF NEW YEAR'S DAY/WORLD FESTIVALS

Breuilly, Elizabeth, Joanne O'Brien, and Martin Palmer. *Festivals of the World: The Illustrated Guide to Celebrations, Customs, Events and Holidays.* Checkmark Books, New York: 2002.

Brunner, Borgna. "A History of the New Year: A Move from March to January." Infoplease. https://www.infoplease.com/calendar-holidays/major-holidays/history-new-year.

"New Year's." History.com, 2010. http://www.history.com/topics/holidays/new-years.

CALENDARS

"History of the Calendar." Infoplease. http://www.infoplease.com/ipa/A0002061.html.

Marie, Niclas. "The History of the Western Calendar." Time Center. https://www.timecenter.com/articles/the-history-of-the-western-calendar/.

"A Variety of Calendars." WebExhibits: Calendars Through the Ages. http://www.webexhibits.org/calendars/calendar.html.

TIMES SQUARE ("MIDNIGHT BALL DROP")

"The Ball Drops Here." Times Square. http://timessquareball.net/.

"New Year's Eve." Times Square. http://www.timessquarenyc.org/events/new-years-eve/index.aspx#.UwVEvfldWCn.

Rolfes, Ellen. "Having a Ball: The History Behind American New Year's Eve Celebrations." PBS Newshour, December 30, 2013. http://www.pbs.org/newshour/rundown/having-a-ball-the-history-behind-american-new-years-eve-celebrations/.

HOGMANAY ("FIRST FOOTING")

Bogle, Lara Suziedelis. "Scots Mark New Year With Fiery Ancient Rites." National Geographic News, December 31, 2002. http://news.nationalgeographic.com/news/2002/12/1230_021231_hogmanay.html.

"Hogmanay." Scotland.org: The official gateway to Scotland. http://www.scotland.org/celebrate-scotland/hogmanay.

"Hogmanay FAQs." Hogmanay.net, November 30, 2015. http://www.hogmanay.net/history/faq.

Lemm, Elaine. "Celebrate Hogmanay, the Scottish New Year Celebration." The Spruce, April 4, 2017. https://www.thespruce.com/hogmanay-new-years-eve-in-scotland-435353.

"New Year's Eve—Hogmanay." Did You Know? Facts About Scotland. http://www.rampantscotland.com/know/blknow12.htm.

RUSSIAN NEW YEARS ("TWO NEW YEARS")

Kubilius, Kerry. "The Russian New Year." About Travel, November 14, 2015. http://goeasteurope.about.com/od/russianculture/a/russiannewyeark.htm.

"The 'Old New Year'—Now That's Something of a Riddle There!" Russian Survey, March 2012. http://www.russian-survey.com/culture-a-customs/106-old-new-year.

Terletski, Michael. "Russian Christmas." Russian Crafts. https://russian-crafts.com/russiantraditions/russian-christmas.html.

Trezza, Matt. "Of Russian Origin: Old New Year." RT: Russiapedia. http://russiapedia.rt.com/of-russian-origin/old-new-year/.

CHINESE NEW YEAR ("DRAGON DANCE")

"Chinese New Year." Topmarks. https://www.topmarks.co.uk/ChineseNewYear/ChineseNewYear.aspx.

"Dragons and the Dragon Dance." One World/Nations Online. http://www.nationsonline.org/oneworld/Chinese_Customs/dragon_dance.htm.

Gong, Rosemary. *Good Luck Life.* New York: HarperCollins, 2005.

Mack, Lauren. "Chinese New Year Guide: Prepare and Celebrate Chinese New Year." About News. http://chineseculture.about.com/od/chinesefestivals/tp/Chinese-New-Year-Guide-Prepare-And-Celebrate-Chinese-New-Year.htm.

Naumann, Sara. "Guide to Celebrating Chinese New Year in Mainland China." About Travel, December 28, 2016. http://gochina.about.com/od/chinesenewyear/p/ChineseNYGuide.htm.

"What Is Dragon Dance?" Gund Kwok. http://gundkwok.org/what-is-dragon-dance/.

NOWRUZ ("THIRTEEN DAYS")

Fulton, April. "Nowruz: Persian New Year's Table Celebrates Spring Deliciously." The Salt/NPR, March 20, 2016. http://www.npr.org/sections/thesalt/2016/03/20/471174857/nowruz-persian-new-years-table-celebrates-spring-deliciously.

Khosraviani, Mahshad. "Happy Nowruz: How We Celebrate the Persian New Year." *The Huffington Post*, May 22, 2013. http://www.huffingtonpost.com/mahshad-khosraviani/happy-nowruz-how-we-celebrate-the-persian-new-year_b_2932545.html.

Michael, Jaclyn. "Celebrating Nowruz: A Resource for Educators." The Outreach Center for Middle Eastern Studies, Harvard University. http://cmes.fas.harvard.edu/files/NowruzCurriculumText.pdf?m=1419359481.

Mindess, Anna. "Persian New Year Welcomes Spring with Symbolic Traditions and Treats." KQED Food, March 12, 2012. http://blogs.kqed.org/bayareabites/2012/03/12/persian-new-year-welcomes-spring-with-symbolic-traditions-and-treats/.

"Norooz, NoRuz, NowRuz: Persian New Year—(Haftsin Table)." FarsiNet. http://www.farsinet.com/noruz/haftsinn4.html.

SONGKRAN ("WASHING THE BAD AWAY")

Bhikkhu, Thanissaro. "Mcrit: A Study Guide." Access to Insight (Legacy Edition), November 30, 2013. http://www.accesstoinsight.org/lib/study/merit.html.

Davidson, Rose. "Songkran." National Geographic Kids. http://kids.nationalgeographic.com/explore/celebrations/songkran/.

Jimmy M. "Songkran 2017 in Bangkok." Bangkok.com. http://www.bangkok.com/information-festivals/songkran.htm.

Rodgers, Greg. "The Thailand Water Festival." About Travel, April 5, 2016. http://goasia.about.com/od/Events-and-Holidays/a/Thailand-Water-Festival.htm.

"Songkran." Thai World View. http://www.thaiworldview.com/feast/songkran.htm.

MUHARRAM ("NEW MOON, NEW YEAR")

"Al Hijra, Ramadan and the Islamic Calendar." Royal Museums Greenwich. http://www.rmg.co.uk/discover/explore/al-hijra-ramadan-and-islamic-calendar.

Ali-Karamali, Sumbul. *Growing Up Muslim.* New York: Delacorte Books, 2012.

Muhammad, Hafiz Abdullah. "The Islamic New Year & the Significance of Muharram." *Islamique* magazine, September 14, 2017. http://islamiquemagazine.com/the-islamic-new-year-the-significance-of-muharram/.

"Muharram/Islamic New Year." Calendar Labs, October 12, 2016. http://www.calendarlabs.com/holidays/india/muharram.php.

Zakkiya. "Explaining Muharram and the Hijri Calendar to Your Kids." Muslim Mommy, November 14, 2012. http://muslimmommy.com/2012/11/14/explaining-muhurram-the-hijrah-calendar-to-your-kids/.

MATARIKI ("BRINGING TOGETHER EARTH AND SKY")

"The Māori." New Zealand in History. http://history-nz.org/maori4.html.

"Matariki—the Aotearoa/Pacific New Year." Christchurch City Libraries. http://my.christchurchcitylibraries.com/matariki/.

"Matariki—Whare Tapere." Museum of New Zealand/Te Papa Tongarewa. https://www.tepapa.govt.nz/learn/matariki-maori-new-year/matariki-whare-tapere.

"Story: Matariki—Māori New Year." The Encyclopedia of New Zealand. http://www.teara.govt.nz/en/matariki-maori-new-year/page-1.

"Traditional Māori Sport and Games." New Zealand in History. http://history-nz.org/kite.html.

WE TRIPANTU ("THE YOUNG SUN RISES")

Bacigalupo, Ana Mariella. *Shamans of the Foye Tree: Gender, Power, and Healing Among Chilean Mapuche.* Austin, TX: University of Texas Press, 2007.

Brook, Jack. "Mapuche Celebrate Winter Solstice." *The Santiago Times*, June 26, 2017. http://santiagotimes.cl/2017/06/26/mapuche-celebrate-winter-solstice-in-chile/.

"Chilean Culture: We Tripantu & the Winter Solstice." Cascada Expediciones, June 21, 2013. https://www.cascada.travel/News/Chilean-Culture-We-Tripantu-Winter-Solstice.

"Chile's Indigenous Mapuche People Celebrate a New Year." Daily Life News, June 23, 2013. http://www.thisischile.cl/8748/2/chiles-indigenous-mapuche-people-celebrate-a-new-year/News.aspx.

"Mapuche Culture." InterPatagonia. https://www.interpatagonia.com/mapuche/index_i.html.

WEP RONPET ("SMASHING THE POTS")

"The Ancient Egyptian New Year: Upet Ronpet." The Virtual Temple of Tutankhamun. http://kemetic-independent.awardspace.us/WepetRonpet.htm.

Sedjfaiemitui. "Year 20 Under Nut, and New Beginnings—Wep Ronpet, the Kemetic New Year." http://warboar.wordpress.com/2012/08/07/wep-ronpet-year-20/.

"Wep Ronpet 2012." The Twisted Rope. http://thetwistedrope.wordpress.com/2012/08/06/wep-ronpet-2012/.

"Wep Ronpet (Kemetic New Year)." Tamara L. Siuda, July 10, 2013. http://tamarasiuda.com/tag/wep-ronpet-kemetic-new-year/.

NAVROZE ("NOWRUZ, NAVROZE")

"India, Parsi Navroz New Year Celebrations." *Parsi News*, April 22, 2010. http://www.parsinews.net/india-parsi-navroz-new-year-celebrations/2068.html.

"Navroz." Zoroastrians.net blog. https://zoroastrians.net/?s=navroz.

"Parsi New Year." Target Study. https://targetstudy.com/knowledge/day/260/parsi-new-year.html.

"Pateti—Parsi New Year Day." Mount View Project Pvt. Ltd. http://mvppl.blogspot.com/2012/08/pateti-parsi-new-year-day.html.

"Zoroastrian Calendar." Zarthoshti Anjuman of Northern California. http://zanc.org/zcal/zcal.html.

ENKUTATASH ("DAISIES")

"Enkutatash (Ethiopian New Year)." News & Events from Around Ethiopia. September 11, 2016. http://ethionetblog.blogspot.com/2011/09/enkutatash-ethiopian-new-year-september.html.

"Enkutatash (Ethiopian New Year): September 11." In Culture Parent, September 7, 2012. http://www.incultureparent.com/2012/09/enkutatash-ethiopian-new-year-september-11/.

"Enkutatash—Ethiopian New Year (September 11)." Awaze Tours. http://www.awazetours.com/Visit-Ethiopia/Ethiopian-Festivals/New_Year.html.

"Ethiopian New Year: Enkutatash." Ethiopian News Agency, September 10, 2016. http://www.ena.gov.et/en/index.php/component/k2/item/1932-ethiopian-new-year-enkutatash.

ROSH HASHANAH ("CASTING AWAY SINS")

"Celebrate Rosh Hashanah." My Jewish Learning. http://www.myjewishlearning.com/category/celebrate/rosh-hashanah/.

Pelala, Ariela. "What Is Rosh HaShanah?" Thought Co., February 23, 2016. https://www.thoughtco.com/what-is-rosh-hashanah-2076484.

Rich, Tracey R. "Rosh Hashanah." Judaism 101. http://www.jewfaq.org/holiday2.htm.

"Rosh Hashanah." History.com, 2009. http://www.history.com/topics/holidays/rosh-hashanah-history.

DIWALI ("FESTIVAL OF LIGHTS")

"Diwali." Kidsgen.com. http://www.kidsgen.com/events/diwali/.

"Diwali." National Geographic Kids. http://kids.nationalgeographic.com/kids/stories/peopleplaces/diwali/.

"Diwali: Festival of Lights." About Religion.com. http://hinduism.about.com/od/diwalifestivaloflights/a/diwali.htm.

"Diwali: The Festival of Lights." Society for the Confluence of Festivals in India (SCFI). http://www.diwalifestival.org/.

"Religions: Diwali." BBC, October 20, 2010. http://www.bbc.co.uk/religion/religions/hinduism/holydays/diwali.shtml.

AÑO VIEJO ("FIRE IS BETTER")

"A Cuenca and Latin American tradition, the New Year's Eve Burning of the año viejo Dummies Clears the Slate for a Better 2016." Cuenca High Life, December 27, 2015. https://cuencahighlife.com/a-latin-american-tradition-the-new-years-eve-burning-of-the-ano-viejo-dummies-clears-the-slate-for-a-better-2014/.

McDowell, Tim. "New Years Eve in Guaranda, Ecuador, and the Año Viejo Effigies." Ecuador Fulbright Guaranda, January 3, 2013. http://ecuadorfulbrightguaranda.wordpress.com/2013/01/03/new-years-eve-in-guaranda-ecuador-and-the-ano-viejo-effigies/.

Meier, Allison. "Spongebob in Flames: The New Year's Eve Effigy Burning in Ecuador." Atlas Obscura, December 31, 2013. http://www.atlasobscura.com/articles/new-years-effigies-ecuador.

NOCHEVIEJA ("LAS DOCE UVAS DE LA SUERTE")

Koehler, Jeff. "Foodways: Green Grapes and Red Underwear: A Spanish New Year's Eve." The Salt/NPR, December 31, 2012. http://www.npr.org/blogs/thesalt/2012/12/26/168092673/green-grapes-and-red-underwear-a-spanish-new-years-eve.

Paula. "The Twelve Lucky Grapes of New Year in Madrid." Sh Madrid/Welcome to Madrid, December 26, 2015. https://www.shmadrid.com/blog/en/the-12-lucky-grapes-of-new-year-in-madrid/.

"Why Do the Spanish Eat 12 Grapes on NYE?" Eye on Spain, December 30, 2016. https://www.eyeonspain.com/blogs/iwonderwhy.aspx?month=201612.